WHITETAIL DEER

Jack Ballard

FALCONGUIDES

GUILFORD, CONNECTICUT
HELENA, MONTANA

FALCONGUIDES®

An imprint of Rowman & Littlefield
Falcon and FalconGuides are registered trademarks and Make Adventure Your Story
is a trademark of Rowman & Littlefield.

Distributed by NATIONAL BOOK NETWORK

Copyright © 2017 Rowman & Littlefield
Photos by Jack Ballard unless otherwise noted.

British Library Cataloguing-in-Publication Information available

Library of Congress Cataloging-in-Publication Data available

ISBN 978-1-4930-2645-6 (paperback)
ISBN 978-1-4930-2646-3 (e-book)

♾™ The paper used in this publication meets the minimum requirements of American National Standard for Information Sciences—Permanence of Paper for Printed Library Materials, ANSI/NISO Z39.48-1992.

This book is dedicated to Larry Cunningham, a friend whose direction and encouragement have been highly instrumental in making my career in writing and photography possible.

Contents

Contents

Chapter 5. Reproduction and Young

Chapter 6. Whitetail Deer and Other Animals

Chapter 7. Whitetail Deer and Humans

Acknowledgments

Swarovski Optics has generously provided superb binoculars to aid my field observations of wildlife. Thank you!

Introduction

At the beginning of my career as a writer, I worked part-time on a ranch west of Missoula, Montana, in exchange for housing for my family and a small herd of cattle. Early one morning, around the first of June, I was checking cattle in a pasture flush with a verdant cover of tall grass. Skirting the meadow, I happened upon a very new whitetail fawn, secreted by its mother at the base of a towering ponderosa pine.

My camera was in the pickup, so I made a hasty retreat to the vehicle. As I lay in a scratchy bed of pine needles 30 feet from the fawn, the rise and fall of its chest was the only thing betraying life in its otherwise motionless form.

For an hour I sprawled in the dirt, taking numerous photos of the newborn. Its rich cinnamon coat punctuated with milky spots was striking, and the camouflage of its form at the base of the reddish, scaly bark of the ancient pine was astonishing. For a brief period, the fawn raised its head, the dark pad on its tiny nostrils twitching, perhaps in response to my own scent.

Some hours later I returned with my young son, planning to show him the fawn. It was gone, whisked away by a mother who had likely detected my scent and taken her offspring to new quarters.

My encounters with whitetail deer have spanned four decades, numerous states, and two countries. Yet when I think of the species, it is that everyday encounter with the fawn that stands uppermost in my memory. Whitetail deer are commonplace to many residents of the United States. But within their familiarity resides a truly remarkable creature. I offer this book in hopes of enhancing the reader's appreciation for the species.

CHAPTER 1 Names and Faces

Names and Visual Description

Whitetail deer are the most widespread hoofed mammal in both North and South America. They are an adaptable, medium-sized deer capable of thriving in a wide range of habitats. They can be found in ecosystems as variable as the burning deserts of Arizona, the swamplands of Alabama, the grasslands of the Dakotas, and the dense evergreen forests in the Rocky Mountains of Idaho. Perhaps it is their broad geographic range and association with people in all of the contiguous United States that leads to some confusion about their name. Scientifically, the species is known as white-tailed deer, but the name "whitetail deer" is also used in professional reference to the species. For example, South Dakota Game, Fish and Parks calls them whitetail deer. Montana, a neighboring state, labels the species as white-tailed deer. In verbiage common to rural areas of the country, these deer may also be referred to as simply whitetails. For the purposes of this book, they will be termed whitetail deer, a preference in nomenclature justified by no more compelling reason than the author's reluctance to endlessly hyphenate the description of the deer's tail. For simplicity's sake, they may also be called whitetails.

When Lewis and Clark returned from their epic journey across the West, they brought with them information regarding a host of animals unknown to folks in the settled portions of the United States. In their journals they often refer to whitetail deer, which they knew in the East as "common deer." At various places in their travels, they encountered and hunted whitetails but described them with different and sometimes confusing names. On the Missouri River in Montana, the expedition killed what Lewis described as "one common fallow or longtailed deer." This was certainly a whitetail, noted in the captain's journal in the same entry, which records the harvest of a mule deer, a separate species. At the Three Forks of the Missouri River (also in Montana) Lewis notes the company did not find any mule deer but hunted "longtailed red deer," which were obviously whitetails. Three decades prior to the Lewis and Clark Expedition, an employee of the Hudson's Bay Company referred to whitetails as "long-tailed jumping deer." Other accounts of the species from the colonial period describe "Virginia deer." This latter nomenclature is reflected in the scientific name for whitetail deer, *Odocoileus virginianus.*

Whitetails are variously colored, with geographical and seasonal differences in their coat colors. Most animals exhibit a rusty-red appearance in the summer when their coats are short and sleek. In early autumn they acquire their winter pelage, which ranges from mostly tan to grayish tan. The slender legs and neck of a whitetail, along with its sculpted head and streamlined torso, give it an athletic appearance. Whitetail deer sport a coal-black nose and hooves. One of their most unique physical features is the appendage from which they get their name. Whitetail deer have a much longer tail than other members of the deer family in North America. The furry tail droops from the rump in an elongated V shape. The visible top side usually matches the color of the deer's body and is edged in white; the tail's underside is completely white. When alarmed, these deer raise their tail, displaying the characteristic white underside. This behavior is the source of the deer's name.

Although the overall impression of a whitetail deer's color is brownish, substantial portions of its body are white or cream colored, including its underside, the insides of the upper portions of its legs, and the rump directly under the tail. Whitetails also sport a patch of white on their throat that extends along the lower jaw in most animals. The insides of a whitetail's ears are white; the tips and edges of the ears are often dark brown or black. Most animals also display two dark spots on the lower jaw toward the rear of the mouth.

Names for whitetails of various ages and genders are the same as those of their close relative, the mule deer. Males are called bucks or less frequently stags. Females are known as does. Young whitetails, from birth to one year of age, are commonly

Whitetail deer are named for the milk-white fur on the underside of their large tail.

referred to as fawns. Animals of both genders from one to two years of age are often dubbed yearlings.

The descriptive term for a male deer is the origin for certain other terms in American culture. A dollar is frequently known in slang as "a buck." This stems from the colonial era, when the hides of deer were highly valued and a staple of trade between Europeans, settlers, and Native Americans. In the late 1700s, a "buckskin," the hide of an adult male whitetail deer, sold for a Spanish dollar, thus the source of a dollar as a buck. The Ohio state tree, the buckeye, also owes its name to an association with whitetail deer. The nut of the buckeye is mostly shiny and reddish, but it contains a duller light-brown spot resembling the shape of a deer's eye. American Indians of the region called the tree *hetuck*, which means "the eye of the buck."

Related Species in North America

Whitetails are part of the deer family of North American mammals that also includes elk, moose, and caribou. They occasionally share range with a less closely related ungulate (hoofed mammal), the pronghorn or antelope. Whitetails are readily distinguished from antelope on the basis of color. Pronghorns exhibit a notable bicolor appearance with the upper part of their body and flanks adorned in reddish brown, their lower ribs, belly, and rump contrasting in white. Both male and female pronghorn have black horns, absent in whitetails, though the horns of female pronghorn are often small and difficult to see.

Moose are much, much bigger than whitetail deer and have a dark brown or blackish coat. The head of a moose is ponderous, highlighted by a large, bulbous nose, and that scarcely resembles the pointed nose and sculpted head of a whitetail. It is unlikely that anyone with a modicum of experience in the outdoors would confuse a moose for a whitetail. Whitetails live in almost all locations inhabited by moose.

Both elk and caribou are notably larger than a whitetail. The coloration is different as well. Elk in summer pelage may be rusty red in appearance, like a whitetail, but the coat on the front

Mule deer (above) and whitetail deer (below) are closely related. Tail size, color, and shape are the best ways to tell them apart. Mule deer have longer ears, a more grayish cast to their fall and winter coats, and usually differently shaped antlers.

shoulders and neck is darker. Their rump is also yellowish in color, unlike a whitetail, and sports just a stub of a tail. Elk and whitetails are found in the same habitat in portions of the East and in numerous locations on the plains and in the Rocky Mountains. Caribou are colored dissimilarly to whitetail deer: Their necks are creamy white while the rest of their body appears in gray tones. Caribou have long hairs along their throat that forms a mane, a characteristic absent in whitetails. Whitetail deer and caribou roam together in parts of Canada, but, with the exception of a few rare interlopers from Canada in the extreme northern reaches of Washington, Idaho, and Montana, whitetails in the contiguous United States never encounter caribou.

The closest relative and the animal most commonly confused with the whitetail is the mule deer. The two deer species share range in numerous locations west of the Mississippi River and sometimes interbreed. Bucks from both species carry antlers. On mature males, it is sometimes possible to distinguish the species by their antler configuration, although this is not a perfect diagnostic tool. The antlers of whitetail deer usually have tines that sprout from a single beam. Mule deer antlers sprout from the head with a main beam that normally forks, then forks again. However, bucks of both species sometimes carry antlers that do not match the common configurations.

Body color and appendage characteristics are the best way to differentiate mule and whitetail deer. The winter coat of a mule deer has a grayish cast, versus the more brownish appearance of most whitetails. In the summer, the two species may both look reddish brown. However, mule deer always sport a creamy rump, with a spindly tail tipped in black. This characteristic in itself is sufficient to distinguish mule deer from whitetails. Additionally, the ears of mule deer are much larger (nearly twice as long) than those of a whitetail.

Subspecies of Whitetail Deer

As with many other species of mammals in North America, the number and classification of various subspecies of whitetail deer is currently a matter of debate among biologists. Worldwide, thirty-eight subspecies of whitetail deer are traditionally recognized. Seventeen of those occur in the United States and Canada. The rest are found in Mexico and Central and South America.

Subspecies were historically classified based on separate geographical ranges and noticeable variations in physical characteristics such as body size, color, and other unique traits including length and shape of appendages or antler size. More recently, taxonomists (scientists who classify animals) have begun to investigate subspecies in relation to genetic differences versus physical characteristics that are sometimes a function of habitat conditions, not true species variation. For example, among deer in Mississippi assumed to belong to a single subspecies, animals from the delta region with fertile soils are 30 to 40 percent heavier than those found in the coastal flatwoods region, which has less productive soils.

Deer management practices during the twentieth century also confound current subspecies classifications. Whitetail deer were hunted to extinction, or nearly to extinction, in numerous regions throughout the United States in the late nineteenth and early twentieth centuries. Deer then were transplanted from one region to another to establish or augment local herds. In 1926, the state of Virginia embarked on an aggressive decades-long translocation program in which deer from other states were released at numerous locations throughout Virginia. Many other states engaged in similar restocking programs. The genetic interchange of these translocation projects has certainly diluted the genetic uniqueness of many supposed subspecies, if such genetic individuality existed in the first place. Research in the past decade has concluded there is no significant difference in the genetic makeup of at least six of the traditionally identified subspecies of whitetails in the United States.

As is the case with other identified subspecies of large mammals in North America, most subspecies of whitetail deer are associated with a specific geographic area. For example, whitetails inhabit several barrier islands along the Atlantic coast. The Hilton Head Island, Bull Island, and Hunting Island subspecies are all found on islands off the coast of South Carolina, isolated populations that presumably migrated at some point from the mainland. Farther south, the Blackbeard Island subspecies ranges only on Blackbeard Island and Sapelo Island near the Georgia coast.

Elsewhere in the country, subspecies have been identified that certainly interbreed due to a lack of geographic barriers between their ranges. The Northwest subspecies and the Dakota subspecies are both claimed to inhabit Montana, the Northwest species found primarily in the western portion of the state, the Dakota subspecies to the east. However, the river corridors favored by whitetail deer contain no natural or man-made barriers to deer dispersion from east to west, so it is safe to conclude these subspecies interbreed in many locations.

Two of the whitetail deer subspecies in the contiguous United States are currently protected under the provisions of the Endangered Species Act (ESA). The Columbian whitetail deer, *Odocoileus virginianus leucurus*, was originally identified along the lower Columbia River and its islands in western Washington. These deer were listed as endangered under the ESA in 1968. In 1978 another small population of Columbian whitetails was identified in southwestern Oregon's Douglas County, and these deer were also listed as endangered. Conservation measures in Oregon led to the growth and expansion of the Douglas County whitetail herd, which was removed from the endangered species list in 2003. In 2013, the United States Fish & Wildlife Service (USFWS) released a status review of the lower Columbia River population that recommended changing their ESA status from endangered to threatened. On October 9, 2015, the USFWS formally proposed the change in status. Since being listed as endangered, the population of whitetails on the lower Columbia River has doubled in number from around 450 animals to 900.

Key deer are the smallest subspecies of whitetails. This young buck is grazing in the National Key Deer Refuge in Florida. Photo courtesy the U.S. Fish and Wildlife Service

The subspecies of North American whitetail deer most distinct from other members of the species is the Key deer. These animals solely inhabit the Florida Keys, a series of tropical islands jutting from the southern tip of Florida. Key deer are notably different from other whitetails for several reasons. First, they are quite tiny in comparison to their northern relatives. While a mature buck in northern Minnesota might weigh over 300 pounds, a 100-pound male Key deer would be considered a giant; average weights for Key deer are 80 pounds for bucks and 62 pounds for does. Key deer fawns normally weigh less than 4 pounds at birth.

Other traits among Key deer are also unique among white-tails. Although they require freshwater to survive, Key deer are highly tolerant of salt water. They have much lower birth rates than other whitetails and tend to be more solitary. Their breed age is older than that observed elsewhere in the species, and the antler development in bucks is slower.

By the early 1950s, Key deer were on the verge of extinction, with only an estimated twenty-five individuals left in the Florida Keys. Overhunting was the primary reason for the decline of Key deer. They received protection from hunting in the early 1950s. In 1967 they were listed as a federally endangered species and are currently listed as endangered by the state of Florida as well. Although the population of Key deer has rebounded significantly since their low, they are still considered vulnerable to extinction by many biologists. The population now numbers nearly one thousand animals, but most of those are found on just two islands, Big Pine Key and No Name Key. Hurricanes, rising sea levels, and disease outbreaks are all disasters that could conceivably wipe out this genetically and geographically isolated population of whitetail deer.

Physical Characteristics

Species that inhabit extended latitudinal ranges tend to exhibit a similarly large range in body mass. Whitetail deer are found from the southernmost portion of the contiguous United States (the Florida Keys) to its northernmost (northern Minnesota), a distance

KEY DEER FACE MULTIPLE RISKS, MANY OF THEM MAN-MADE

The recovery of Key deer from a couple dozen animals in the 1950s to nearly one thousand in 2015 is a wildlife success story in the making. However, Key deer face multiple risks to their health and survival, many of them directly created by humans. Loss of habitat through residential and other development on the Florida Keys is one problem. Vehicles are another; collisions with vehicles are a major source of mortality for Key deer. They may also develop digestive problems by eating trash from unsecured garbage bins. Domestic dogs sometimes injure or kill deer. Uninformed people feeding deer is another major problem. Key deer utilize over one hundred natural food sources on the islands. They do not need human food, and the practice of feeding them increases dependency on unnatural food sources and decreases their natural, healthy aversion to people.

spanning 1,650 miles. Following a biological rule that body mass increases from south to north, Key deer are the smallest in the country; those dwelling in northern Minnesota are among the largest. Buck deer in Minnesota usually range from 100 to 300 pounds in weight; some males get even heavier. Minnesota does normally range from 85 to 130 pounds. Nationwide, the average weights for whitetail bucks and does are around 140 and 100 pounds, respectively. Occasionally, both bucks and does achieve sizes much larger than average. In 1926 a Minnesota hunter killed a whitetail buck that, after its internal organs were removed, weighed 402 pounds. Officials from the state's Department of

Whitetails living in colder northern climates are notably larger on average than deer found farther south.

Conservation estimated the buck had a live weight of 511 pounds. It is assumed by many to be the heaviest whitetail buck on record.

In most of their habitat in the United States and Canada, adult whitetail deer stand about 2.5 to 3.5 feet at the shoulder. The length of their body from nose to tail is commonly 6 to 7 feet. Because the neck and head of a whitetail extend above its shoulders, the typical adult deer's total height is about shoulder level to the average human female.

Antlers and Antler Development

Whitetail bucks grow antlers, bony appendages from their head that may be used for defense against aggressors, in dominance battles with other bucks, and as a symbol of a buck's vigor to both other males and females of his kind. In rare cases, does with hormonal abnormalities may also develop antlers; in wild populations, about one in three thousand does will have some form of antler development. Antlers sprout from bony projections on the frontal bones of the skull known as pedicles. Pedicles are similar in shape to a nearly rhyming word, "pedestal." In fact, the relationship between pedicles and pedestals can be helpful in understanding antler development. Pedicles appear as bony pedestals thrusting from a buck's skull. Similar to the common phrase "he fell off his pedestal," a buck's antlers detach from the pedicle every year. Antlers are thus described as deciduous, meaning they are regrown every year like the leaves on a deciduous tree.

Pedicles are noticeable on buck fawns by the time they reach four to five months of age. These bony nubs are often called buttons and are found on the top of the fawn's skull between his eyes and ears. As the buck ages, his pedicles tend to shorten but become broader, allowing subsequent antlers to achieve a larger diameter at the base.

Growing antlers are called velvet antlers for their fuzzy, velvety appearance. The velvet on the outside of the antlers forms a thin skin over the antlers, which are composed of bone. This skin is filled with an extensive system of blood vessels that provide nutrients to the rapidly growing antlers. At maximal expansion antlers on a whitetail buck may grow up to 0.5 inch per day. Antlers in the growth stage are formed of soft tissue that turns to bone through a process of calcification that occurs toward the end of yearly antler development. In late summer, shifting hormones cause the blood supply to diminish. The velvet then sloughs from the antlers, a process that is often aided by whitetail bucks rubbing their antlers on trees and shrubs. Naturally colored white, the antlers soon take on various shades of brown. The coloration comes from staining and foreign material on the antlers. Bucks that rub their antlers on various types of trees may develop antlers that range in color from nearly white to a deep, chocolate brown. In some habitats whitetail antlers are more reddish than brown.

Antler size is a function of a buck's age, genetics, and nutrition. Studies on antler development indicate a buck will maximize

This Smoky Mountain National Park buck's antlers are in the "velvet" stage. The deer was photographed in early summer. LISA BALLARD

Antler size is locally correlated with a buck's age, but the number of tines on a buck's antlers does not tell his age. This buck in Shenandoah National Park has ten points on his antlers, but other physical features indicate he is half that age, at the oldest.

his potential for antler growth at about six years of age. Some research suggests the timing of a buck's birth and the body condition of his mother during gestation also have lasting effects on antler size. Yearling bucks carry a set of antlers bearing about 30 percent of their maximal size. The antlers on two-year-olds achieve about 60 percent, three-year-olds 80 percent. From three to six years of age, antler size increases more slowly. Bucks may carry antlers at or near their maximum size for several years after their peak, if they remain free from injury and have access to adequate nutrition.

The overall size and number of tines (or points) on a buck's antlers increase with age. Can you tell a buck's age by counting the number of tines on his antlers? While some erroneously believe this theory, it is not true. Yearling bucks usually have spike antlers that consist of a single, elongated tine or exhibit two tines, in which case they are often called forkhorns. A few bucks may only carry two tines on each antler on their second set of antlers; others may have up to five. It is thus impossible to assess a buck's age based on his number of antler points. However, if an observer is familiar with the growth patterns of bucks in a particular region, age can be roughly estimated by antler mass (circumference) and overall length.

Whitetail bucks shed their antlers every year before growing a new set from the pedicles. Older bucks with larger antlers shed theirs first, usually in mid- to late winter. Complex hormone interactions regulate the shedding of antlers. The level of testosterone, a male hormone, declines dramatically in the winter. This causes the adhesion of the antlers to the pedicles to decrease until the weight of the antlers pulls them from the buck's head. Once one antler falls from a buck with a large rack, its head is immediately unbalanced. If the buck then shakes its head, the other antler often falls as well. In many cases, the cast antlers of mature whitetail bucks are found in close proximity to each other.

As testosterone levels begin to rise in the spring, the adhesion of the growing antlers to the pedicles becomes very strong. This bond is so tenacious that hardened antlers will break before being pulled loose from the pedicle, a condition that persists until the antlers are cast the following winter.

CHAPTER 2 Range and Habitat

North American Range—Historic

Whitetail deer historically were animals of the woodlands and waterways of North America. They thrive in many geographical locations and habitat types but are found most consistently where woodland cover is interspersed with open areas. Whitetails are often described as animals of the edges, meaning places where forest cover intersects with meadows or other treeless space, offering them the best opportunity to thrive.

Prior to European settlement in what is now the contiguous United States, most of the territory east of the Mississippi

Whitetails are often described as animals of the edges. They thrive where cover is interspersed with more open areas.

River was forested and home to whitetail deer. American Indians hunted deer, utilizing their flesh for food, their bones for various implements, and their hide for clothing and shelter. These intelligent, enterprising hunters realized whitetails were found most frequently in transitional areas of the forest and sometimes deliberately set fire to the woodlands to create open areas with newly grown vegetation to attract deer and other animals. The diminutive Key deer of Florida were present prior to European settlement, their population already isolated by geography from deer on the mainland.

Whitetails were also found west of the Mississippi River during precolonial times, but the extent of their range and the density of their populations in this part of the country are often a matter of speculation. The species is known to have inhabited river corridors across the West in good numbers. They were also found on streams flowing to the Pacific Ocean on the west side of the Continental Divide.

In the Southwest, whitetail deer roamed across the Texas hills and river bottoms. Archaeological evidence shows deer were an extremely important part of the diet of the native peoples of Texas and Oklahoma for several millennia prior to European or Spanish settlement. The Coues whitetail deer of New Mexico and Arizona, one of the subspecies of whitetails identified in the United States, thrive in timbered areas at higher elevations than the desert scrub. These deer are notably small compared to their northern counterparts. They are believed to be the remnants of a whitetail population that became isolated when changing climate and habitat conditions eliminated forestlands at lower elevations, effectively separating these animals from their kin elsewhere in the region.

Historical biology of whitetail numbers and distribution in the United States indicates the species began to decline in the 1700s. Pressure from hunting by newly arrived Europeans and increased harvest by native hunters who acquired firearms both played a role in decreasing whitetail numbers in the East. Some biologists believe there may have been a short-term uptick in whitetail

Whitetails can thrive in quite arid environments. This bounding buck was photographed in central Texas.

numbers in the early 1800s, a period of time when logging and clearing of land for agricultural purposes improved habitat for deer in numerous places east of the Mississippi River.

From around 1850 to 1900, whitetail populations contracted dramatically. It is impossible to know how many deer existed before Europeans came to North America. One common estimate puts the population in 1450 in what is now the United States at around thirty million animals. By 1900 that number had plummeted to less than three hundred thousand animals, according to some estimates. Regardless of the actual number, whitetail deer had been completely eliminated or their ranks drastically reduced in many parts of the country.

Two major factors contributed to the plunge in populations. First, an active market for deer meat and hides motivated people to hunt deer for profit. Secondly, improvements in firearms made killing deer more efficient. Repeating rifles, capable of firing several cartridges without being reloaded, allowed hunters greater capacity for downing multiple deer in a single episode or repeat shots at deer they missed. This technology, coupled with market demand, unregulated hunting, and an ever-growing human population in the United States prompted a crash in whitetail deer numbers in the closing decades of the nineteenth century.

Legal protections for deer were enacted in most states in the first two decades of the twentieth century. These consisted mainly of hunting seasons that made it illegal to kill deer outside of this time period and regulated how many deer and what sex could be harvested. Conservation measures, such as the creation of habitat reserves, were also gaining popularity with citizens concerned about whitetail deer and other wildlife.

But the dearth of deer was critical across many regions that now hold some of the nation's most robust herds of whitetails. By 1904, whitetails had been completely eliminated in the state of Ohio. Whitetail numbers in Missouri had plummeted to around four hundred, according to a 1925 estimate. In 1898 the state of Iowa completely closed its deer-hunting season due to the fact whitetails were rarely sighted and had been completely eliminated in most of the state. Whitetails were extinct in Kansas and Indiana by the early 1920s.

Whitetail deer populations began a slow recovery in most regions by the 1920s. Lands cleared for agriculture and logging created the edge and clearing habitat favored by deer. The Great Depression was also helpful for whitetails. As citizens fled small farms and rural areas to seek work in the cities, the abandoned land they left behind became refuges for wildlife.

From the 1950s to 2000, whitetail deer numbers increased about as rapidly as they dropped in the second half of the nineteenth century. Translocation programs (moving deer from one site to another) enhanced or established populations of whitetails

Many experts feel there are now as many or more whitetails in North America than in precolonial times.

in scores of locations. Management of deer numbers through hunting seasons and conservation efforts, often funded by revenue from hunting licenses, led to an increased amount of protected habitat. Today it is estimated there are some thirty million whitetail deer in the United States. Most experts believe there are now as many or perhaps more whitetails in the country as in precolonial times.

The historic range of whitetail deer covered much of North America and was probably similar to the species' range today. While the distribution of many North American ungulates (such as bighorn sheep) is currently much smaller than it was in historic times, whitetail deer have possibly increased the extent of their range in comparison to the presettlement era.

North American Range—Current

Whitetail deer inhabit the United States and Canada to the extent that it is easier to describe their range in terms of where they are not found than where they are present. As of 2016, only two states are devoid of resident whitetail populations: California and Nevada. It is possible that deer from Oregon and Idaho occasionally make their way into these states, but there is no official record of a reproducing population.

Utah was also officially devoid of whitetails until the tail end of the twentieth century. Sightings of whitetail deer were reported in the northern part of the state beforehand, but the first documented whitetail was located in Cache County, in the north-central region, in 1996. In 2000, wildlife officials recorded the killing (legal) of a whitetail deer by a hunter. In the past two decades, whitetails have become permanent residents of the state in an expanding population occurring primarily northwest of the Great Salt Lake. It is expected that whitetails will continue to expand their range southward and into other river-bottom and agricultural areas of the state in the future. Wildlife officials estimate there are now over one thousand whitetail deer in Utah.

Whitetails are mostly absent in New Mexico and Arizona, with the exception of the Coues subspecies. Coues deer range across the mountains of southwestern New Mexico and are found in Arizona in mountainous territory in the south-central and southeastern portions of the states from the Mexico border northward through the Tucson area. The Flagstaff area represents the northern end of whitetail deer range in Arizona.

Oregon contains relatively few whitetail deer in three distinct populations. The Columbian whitetail (discussed under Subspecies of Whitetail Deer in chapter 1) is found in two rather small areas: the extreme northwest corner of the state along the Columbia River and in southwestern Oregon in Douglas County. Whitetails are also present in the northeast as part of a connected population to Idaho and Washington (Washington holds whitetails in most of the western half of the state). They are located primarily in Wallowa, Union, and Baker Counties.

In the remainder of the contiguous United States, whitetail deer are broadly distributed in relation to viable habitat. Overall, their range is expanding, particularly in western states. In the Rocky Mountains, whitetail deer now occupy higher percentages of mountain habitat and at higher elevations than seen in previous decades. For example, in November 2004, a park biology crew observed a whitetail doe in Colorado's Rocky Mountain National Park at an elevation of 8,630 feet. I have personally witnessed whitetail deer on the spine of the Continental Divide on the Montana-Idaho border at 6,600 feet and at nearly 8,000 feet in the Snowcrest Mountains of Montana. Whitetail deer have also increased their distribution in the semiarid prairie lands of several western states in the past few decades.

Perhaps the most dramatic aspect of whitetail deer range expansion is seen on Canada's northern frontier. Many biologists have noted the continuing northern movement of whitetail range in various portions of Canada in the last few decades. In western Canada, small bands of deer are now found in the southern portion of the Northwest Territories and appear to be moving slowly north. A hunter harvested a whitetail doe in good health about 65 miles south of the Arctic Circle in 1996. Climate change, and the habitat alterations it produces, will likely facilitate an even farther-northward expansion of the profoundly adaptable whitetail deer in the future.

Whitetail Deer Habitat

Whitetail deer are considered one of the most adaptable ungulates in North America. They thrive in a broad range of geographic areas and habitats, but one necessity restricts their distribution: water. Whitetails will rarely be found more than a mile from a consistent water source.

A wide range of plants, shrubs, and trees can be utilized by whitetail deer for food. But a key component of their habitat is cover, generally composed of shrubs or trees that deer use to hide from humans and other predators. Whitetails also use cover for protection from winds and precipitation in the fall and

Whitetail deer are rarely found more than a mile from water.

winter, and they retreat to shaded areas to escape heat during the summer.

The necessity of cover for whitetails is readily observed in areas characterized by sprawling cultivation for agriculture. Crops such as soybeans, corn, alfalfa, and wheat represent attractive food sources for deer. However, if some woody cover is not present, deer will be found in low numbers or absent entirely. In heavily farmed areas, hedgerows and ravines unfit for cultivation that hold trees and shrubs provide deer enough cover to thrive. Numerous studies have shown that although deer can live with less, areas containing at least 30 percent cover represent the best habitat for whitetails.

"Forest succession" is the term used to describe the process of forest growth from infancy to maturation. Infant forests are

Whitetails thrive in agricultural areas, which often support very high deer densities.

those where some natural (fire, hurricane, flood) or man-made (logging, clearing for agriculture) occurrence has killed all or most of the trees in an area. In the early stages of forest succession, grasses, broad-leaved plants, and fast-growing shrubs and trees dominate the landscape. As larger deciduous and evergreen trees take over, the forest canopy closes, eliminating most direct sunlight from the forest floor. The understory becomes more barren. As the forest ages, fewer large trees dominate. The canopy opens somewhat, allowing enough sunlight to support a moderate level of lower-growing shrubs and plants to develop at ground level.

Whitetail deer thrive in habitats at the early stages of forest succession. These provide abundant food during all seasons of

URBAN HABITATS— POSSIBILITIES AND PERILS

In the past several decades, a novel habitat has seen an explosion in whitetail deer numbers. Urban and suburban areas are now home to thousands upon thousands of whitetail deer. The growth of deer populations in urban environments stems from two sources. First, as suburbs sprawl into forested and agricultural areas, they increasingly encompass land already inhabited by deer. Secondly, some deer have moved into suburban areas from the wildlands, apparently attracted to consistent food sources and protection from hunting and predators.

A few deer in town are usually seen as cute. Too many are destructive to landscaping, increase deer-vehicle collisions, and may contribute to the spread of disease, most notably Lyme disease, which is carried by the deer tick.

How to manage urban deer is often contentious. Lethal suppression through tightly controlled hunting or sharpshooting programs are most effective but are frequently protested by animal rights activists. Nonlethal removal through trapping and relocating is very expensive, as are programs that attempt to contain numbers through some form of birth control.

For over a century, state wildlife agencies focused their resources on managing whitetail deer in rural and wild environments. Increasingly, deer managers and biologists are being forced to deal with deer in their own backyards.

Urban areas frequently support numerous whitetail deer, often creating challenges for wildlife managers and residents. Dominic Ballard

the year. They also benefit from mature, old-growth forests. In the East, the large trees of mature woodlands provide mast (nuts and fruit) that represent excellent food sources in the fall. Mature forests yield both protection from the elements during the winter months and woody plants upon which the deer may browse. Middle-aged evergreen forests, characterized by dense, light-blocking stands of species such as pine and fir, offer little for deer to eat. In woodlands, areas where infant forests are developing adjacent to mature timber offer whitetails the perfect mix of habitat.

CHAPTER 3 Nutritional Requirements and Forage

Nutritional Requirements

It is sometimes noted that the basic nutritional requirements for a grown whitetail buck are similar to those of an adult man. The buck needs about the same number of calories during a day as the man, but the food sources and the process by which they are digested are very different.

As a general rule, an adult deer consumes about 5 percent of its body weight in forage per day. Thus, a delicate adult doe in Florida's Everglades National Park weighing 90 pounds eats only about 4 to 5 pounds for forage per day, while a strapping buck in Virginia's Shenandoah National Park weighing 180 pounds eats around 9 pounds of food per day. However, food consumption for deer varies by nutritional quality and availability. When attractive forage is essentially limitless, as it is for whitetails with access to desired agricultural crops, animals may eat 7 percent of their body weight per day. Deer subsisting on woody browse will have to ingest more feed than those with access to nutritious broad-leaved plants.

The food requirements change over time, following a consistent pattern dependent on the age and reproductive status of the animal and the season of the year. An adult deer that is not pregnant, nursing a fawn, or growing antlers can maintain a healthy body with 6 to 10 percent protein in its diet. A growing fawn needs 14 to 18 percent protein for average growth; maximal growth for fawns is achieved when they receive 16 to 20 percent dietary protein.

Adult bucks that are growing antlers and pregnant does need nearly double the protein to maintain optimal health as they do at other times of the years. Lactating does (those nursing fawns) also require about twice as much protein, as they are converting

This foraging buck in Shenandoah National Park consumes about the same number of calories per day as an adult man.

Does nursing fawns require higher levels of protein to maintain their health.

protein from plants into the protein-rich, nutrient-laden milk that nourishes their fawns. Numerous studies have found that antler growth in bucks is highly related to good nutrition. One study of domestic deer found that two-year-old bucks eating a diet containing 16 percent protein grew antlers that had twice as much mass as those consuming 8 percent protein. In this case, the bucks needed protein for both antler growth and body development, as males normally do not reach their full body weight until four years of age.

Deer also need a variety of minerals in their diet. Two important minerals are calcium and phosphorous. These are needed for reproduction, bone development, and antler growth. Hardened antlers contain around 11 percent phosphorous and 22 percent

Bucks with developing antlers, like this one in Great Smoky Mountains National Park, need mineral- and protein-rich forage to nourish the growing tissue. LISA BALLARD

calcium. Both does and bucks concentrate these minerals in their bones. At times when other parts of the body (such as growing antlers or a developing fetus) need more of these minerals than the deer consumes in food, the minerals may be temporarily "borrowed" from the bones, then restored later.

Water is another crucial element in the nutrition of a whitetail. Deer may gain a significant amount of their needed moisture from plants, but in most places they still need surface water to survive, at least during certain times of the year. Water intake varies by season and geographic region. The exact water requirements of whitetails aren't fully understood, but most experts believe deer need 2 to 3 quarts of water per day for every 100 pounds of body weight. Most of whitetails' favorite foods are quite high in moisture. Apples, for example, are a treat for deer and hold about 80 percent moisture. Acorns, another favored food, contain about 70 percent moisture.

The water in forage reduces the amount of surface water a deer needs from a pond or stream, but most whitetails still drink water regularly. In arid environments, reliable water sources are a requirement for deer. Rarely will a whitetail go longer than forty-eight hours without drinking. In the winter, deer eat snow to obtain moisture. Deer that browse on vegetation moistened by rain or dew also gain moisture along with the feed.

Digestion

Deer belong to a class of animals known as ruminants or "cud chewers." Other ruminants include cattle, bison, elk, pronghorn,

Whitetails consume forage, then regurgitate and chew it while resting. This bedded doe is chewing her cud.

and sheep. Most ruminants have four stomachs, but some, like the camel, have three. Whitetail deer have four stomachs: the rumen, the reticulum, the omasum, and the abomasum. Ruminants eat quickly, minimally chewing their food before swallowing. At a later time, it is regurgitated and re-chewed to aid digestion. The food regurgitated from the rumen is called cud.

The first chamber of the stomach, the rumen, is the largest and normally holds about 80 percent of the solid mass in a deer's digestive system. Biologists theorize that deer consume most of their food in short bouts to counter predation. The distractive process of eating is minimized. Chewing, via the cud, usually takes place when the animals are resting and can be more vigilant to danger.

After the cud is chewed to a finer texture, it passes from the rumen through the other three stomachs of a whitetail, where it is further broken down. Nutrients are absorbed in the deer's stomachs, but the bulk of the energy and nutrition is extracted from the small intestine, where the food passes after leaving the abomasum, the last of the four stomachs.

Interestingly, the digestive system of the whitetail adapts to the type and amount of food it is eating. The rumen is essentially a fermentation chamber, where a multitude of microorganisms feed upon the forage a deer has swallowed, further breaking it down and converting it to more digestible molecules. The rumen is lined with tiny tendrils known as papillae. Papillae extend when the deer is eating nutrient-packed green forage in the spring and contract in autumn, when woody browse composes more of the diet. The composition of the "soup" in a deer's rumen changes with the seasons as well. In early spring, winter-stressed deer may starve to death with a full stomach because the digestive slurry has not yet adapted to breaking down green forage.

Food Sources

Whitetail deer take advantage of a dizzying array of food sources. If variety is the spice of life, there are few creatures that lead a more savory existence than deer. Studies of feeding deer in Missouri have revealed whitetails consume more than 600 different species of plants. Similar studies in arid climates in southwestern states have shown an equally high number of plants consumed by deer. Research in Arizona indicates whitetail deer eat at least 610 different plant species statewide.

Because it would take the entire contents of a book to catalog all the plants a whitetail might eat, it's easier to understand their food sources in broad categories that apply to different geographic regions and habitats. Probably the favorite type of forage for whitetail deer is forbs. In its widest definition, a forb is a flowering plant that dies aboveground each year and doesn't belong to the family of grasses or rushes. Forbs, like clover, occur in natural habitat and are also found as agricultural crops such as alfalfa. They develop at various times during the growing season, but most sprout and grow quickly during the spring. Many forbs are very nutritious and contain more protein than other plants.

In a natural habitat, browse is another extremely important and desirable food source for whitetails. Browse refers to the leaves, shoots, buds, and other parts of plants whose stems remains aboveground in winter. Browsing is most strongly associated with shrubs and trees. In many part of North America, browse is the primary food source for deer in the winter and plays an important role in whitetail nutrition at other times of the year. Deciduous trees such as maples, aspens, oaks, and dogwood are eaten by whitetails, in addition to many other species. Chokecherry, blueberry, snowberry, and honeysuckle are among a host of shrubs readily consumed by deer. Evergreen browse is also an important food in some places, especially during winter.

Grasses tend to be a lesser food source for whitetail deer, but they are eaten in fairly high quantities in some places at certain times of the year. The tender, greening grasses of spring are happily munched by whitetails. Sufficient rain also causes green regrowth of some grass species in the fall. These may offer a source of nutritious, tender forage for deer at a time of year when it is quite scarce.

Browse in the form of twigs and bark from deciduous trees is an important dietary item for many whitetails. This buck is nipping browse from a cottonwood tree.

"Mast" is a term used to describe the fruit and nuts from a variety of trees and shrubs. Mast is a preferred food for whitetails during the fall. Nuts and fruit provide large amounts of energy and nutrition, and they help whitetails develop fat reserves needed to survive cold winters. Deer love apples, berries, persimmons, grapes, and other fruits. In the desert Southwest, the pods of honey mesquite trees are an important mast crop, especially in drought years. Whitetails eat a wide assortment of berries when available, such as huckleberries, raspberries, and blackberries.

Acorns and other nuts are an exceedingly important mast crop for whitetails in many places. When abundant, acorns may compose more than 70 percent of a whitetail's diet in the fall.

Whitetails sometimes eat aquatic vegetation. This doe is feeding on submerged vegetation at the National Bison Range in Montana.

Studies in Tennessee and Georgia have indicated a strong correlation between the body weights of young deer and acorn production. Reproduction rates in young animals also appear to be higher in some regions when acorns are plentiful.

Other food sources less commonly eaten but sometimes locally important include aquatic plants, lichens, fungi, and ferns. Whitetails are even known at times to chew on dead fish and insects.

KILLED BY COMPASSION

It's a human tendency to care for things we value. When people observe skinny deer suffering during a difficult winter, they may be inclined to offer them feed. Other individuals may be motivated to offer deer a handout whenever it gets cold, believing they are doing the animals a favor.

However, biologists discourage feeding deer for a variety of reasons. Feeding tends to concentrate deer in small areas, greatly increasing the potential for disease transmission. Dominant deer—those best able to survive the winter—get most of the feed, leading to a situation where those who need it the most (such as fawns) receive little benefit. Feeding deer in urban areas often creates travel corridors across roads, where injury and automobile damage are likely to occur.

In some cases, deer are literally killed by feeding. Introducing attractive food sources such as alfalfa hay that the digestive system of a starving deer isn't prepared to accept can accelerate its starvation. Any sudden change in diet in the winter can cause health problems. Deer given grain may develop acidosis (too much acid in the rumen) or experience debilitating diarrhea.

Whitetails have adapted over thousands of years to handle winter. The species will remain the healthiest without our help.

Migration

Mention the term "migration" and few people will associate it with whitetail deer. However, whitetails migrate regularly in some areas, sometimes at surprisingly long distances.

Whitetail migrations occur in two different patterns, with individual animals often following one or the other. Some deer are obligate migrators, meaning they migrate every year, no matter what the weather or habitat conditions. Others are conditional migrators, referring to animals that migrate some years but not others, depending on the conditions. In some populations, individual deer may be obligate migrators, conditional migrators, or nonmigratory. Researchers in southern Minnesota have found deer following all three patterns in the same area.

In the Midwest and other areas of widespread, intense agriculture, deer migrate in relation to crop growth and harvest. Growing crops provide whitetails with forage. Taller crops such as corn also give them a place to hide. Once the crops are harvested in the late summer or fall, the deer lose both their food source and cover. This prompts deer to move to areas where cover is present, sometimes triggering a migration of several miles.

Whitetails in northern habitats, including places like the Adirondack Mountains of New York or the forests of northern Minnesota and Michigan, are often migratory. In northern Minnesota, researchers have documented whitetail migrating over 30 miles. Migrations in these areas often lead deer to wintering areas known as yards, where many deer spend the winter in a relatively small area. As snow depth increases, travel becomes difficult. Yarding deer create trails that make for easier movement.

In migratory populations, cold and snow depth—or more often, some combination thereof—are the triggers that spur deer to move from summer to winter range. A study conducted in the Dakotas concluded that whitetails may migrate 7 miles or sometimes notably farther between their summer and winter ranges. For these deer, temperature appears to the primary impetus for changing residence. Migration is initiated when daytime temperatures remain below freezing for three consecutive days, a

Deep snow and cold temperatures can prompt whitetail migrations. Some migrate every year; others move only during severe winters.

situation that is often encountered during a major storm event. If temperatures rise after an initial migration occurs, the deer remaining on summer range sometimes stay until another cold snap initiates another migratory wave. Another study in southern Minnesota documented whitetail migrations beginning when temperatures dropped below 20 degrees Fahrenheit. Some studies conducted in the Adirondack Mountains in northern New York have concluded that migrations toward wintering areas occurred with lowering temperatures but were also spurred when snow depths reached around 14 inches.

Spring migrations in whitetail deer populations tend to follow the development of food sources. As snow melts and seasonal plants begin to develop, whether naturally or via agriculture, deer follow these food sources between their summer and winter ranges.

CHAPTER 4

Abilities and Behavior

Physical Abilities

Whitetail deer are widely believed to be the most adaptable ungulate in North America. Their diet is unspecialized, and their bodies can adjust to the demands of living in a broad range of habitats. But another factor in their capacity to thrive in such a diversity of living quarters is their remarkable physical abilities.

Information regarding the running speeds of animals is readily available from online and other sources, but it is wildly

Whitetails in full flight may reach speeds over 35 miles per hour. Recognizing their superior speed, predators seldom attempt to catch a fleeing deer from a distance.

inconsistent. Whitetails are commonly reported as reaching a top speed between 30 and 47 miles per hour. Which is it?

It appears that when reporting animal speeds, many sources provide unverified information from other sources that is based upon some assumed expert's best estimate. I know of no formal testing of wild animals' speeds. Probably the best information results in situations where a vehicle has inadvisably chased an animal or is driving parallel to a running animal. Several accounts report vehicles clocking whitetails at just over 40 miles per hour in maximum flight. Under most conditions, whitetail deer are probably capable of briefly sprinting at around 35 miles per hour. Normal running speeds are thought to be about 25 miles per hour.

The gait of a whitetail is often described as bounding. With each bound the deer thrusts itself forward with the large muscles in its hindquarters. Its body extends until its rear hooves both leave the ground and are pointed directly behind the animal. At maximum extension in the bound, there is nearly a straight line from the deer's extended rear hooves along its belly to its front hooves, which are thrust forward in front of its body. The deer then engages its back and other muscles to arc its spine and pull its hind legs slightly ahead of its front hooves when they return to the ground. This allows a whitetail to propel itself incredibly long distances with each bound. Whitetail deer have been measured spanning over 25 feet in a single jump. The notable speed of whitetails enables them to elude all but the most enduring or stealthy predators.

Another remarkable ability of whitetail deer is their jumping prowess. Deer love many types of garden vegetables and ornamental plants. Will a 6-foot fence protect your corn and lettuce from whitetails? Probably not, if the deer is really craving a snack. Whitetail deer can clear an 8-foot fence with some effort. Dr. Leonard Lee Rue, one of the leading whitetail experts and authors in the United States, reports personally witnessing whitetails jumping 9.5-foot fences.

This buck hops a 4-foot fence with ease. Whitetails can leap over obstacles more than twice that high, if necessary.

Their leaping ability, however, is not just used for raiding gardens. Whitetails fleeing a predator such as a coyote or wolf can use obstacles like fallen trees or brush piles to slow their pursuers. In such cases the deer bounds over the obstacle, forcing the predator to run around it. I have seen and observed the tracks of whitetails clearing tangles of downed timber measuring about 6 feet high and at least 6 feet wide.

The strength of the whitetail's limbs is put to another use then eluding predators. Whitetail deer are remarkably strong swimmers. It is commonly reported that they can swim up to 13

Whitetails are very strong swimmers. These deer are swimming on a lake between an island and the mainland in New York's Adirondack Park.

miles per hour, though that figure appears to be based on a single, anecdotal incident when an individual purportedly clocked a swimming doe against his motorboat's tachometer. At that pace, a deer could cover a mile in the water in less than five minutes. Other estimates put the normal swimming speed of whitetails at around 4 to 5 miles per hour.

Regardless of their top speed, whitetails are very comfortable in the water and readily swim to elude predators. Where states or hunting district boundaries are separated by rivers, whitetail deer often swim from one location to another to avoid human hunters. Acclaimed naturalist Ernest Thompson Seton records an incident of a whitetail deer being found at sea, 5 miles from the coast of Maine in his book *The Life Histories of Northern Animals*, published in 1909. There are other accounts of whitetails swimming more than a mile off the Atlantic coast, and deer have been observed crossing large lakes in the United States and Canada.

Strong muscles help whitetails swim, but other aspects of their physical biology are also helpful. The hair of deer is hollow and buoyant, especially the longer, denser hair of their winter coat. Fat stored under the skin and around internal organs also aids in a deer's ability to float with ease. Fat and fur also combine to keep deer warm in cold water temperatures that would be debilitating to a human swimmer without protective gear.

As predator-avoiding strategies, the running and swimming prowess of the whitetail is only as good as the animal's capability in detecting a threat. Whitetail deer have superb senses that work together to inform them of the presence of other creatures in various settings. In open country, the keen eyesight of a whitetail is normally its best sense for identifying a predator. In dense forests, the deer may be more dependent on its ultrasensitive nose or excellent hearing to discern a threat. Singly or in combination, the acute, adaptable senses of whitetails are one of the reasons they are able to thrive in such an expansive array of habitats.

It is often said that the vision of deer is much better than the eyesight of people, but such a statement depends on one's definition of "better." The shape and composition of a deer's eyeball is

Eyes set on the sides of their head give whitetails an expansive field of vision.

quite different than a person's. It has been known for a long time that, compared to the round pupil of the human eye, the whitetail's pupil is shaped like a horizontal slit. A recent research project involving observations and computer modeling at the University of California–Berkeley demonstrates the shape of a deer's pupil is very effective in detecting motion and other visual cues at ground level, and helps in blocking overhead, dazzling light that sometimes confounds vision. The study also found that deer can rotate their eyeballs at least 50 degrees, about ten times farther than a human. This allows deer and other grazing animals with similarly shaped eyes to rotate their eyes upward when they drop their heads to graze or feed near the ground to maintain visual vigilance against predators.

Another aspect of whitetail eyesight that greatly assists them in evading predators is their exceptionally large field of vision. The eyes of a deer are set on the sides of its head, allowing for a field of vision spanning over 300 degrees. This allows deer to detect motion to the sides and even toward the rear of their bodies. Compared to a human's 180-degree field of vision, this aspect of whitetail eyesight gives them a much better ability to see objects a person or canine predator could only detect by swiveling its head.

In the past decade, several groundbreaking research studies have been conducted that indicate other significant differences between the vision of whitetail deer and humans. Deer have a poor capacity to discern detail. It is estimated that for general detail-oriented vision, whitetails are similar to a human with 20/200 vision or someone who can see but is legally blind because his or her vision is blurred. It also appears that deer have a horizontal band of sight in which they can detect greater detail. This might be likened to a computer screen where the middle 20 percent of the screen is in reasonably sharp focus but blurs quickly toward the top and bottom.

Whitetails also see color much differently than people. Research has demonstrated that deer detect only part of the color spectrum seen by humans. Whereas deer see blue tones exceptionally well (on the short wavelength side of the spectrum), they do not detect red (on the long wavelength side). Human eyes have a colored pigment in the lens that blocks ultraviolet radiation; deer do not. This has led some researchers to believe whitetails have the capacity for vision in the ultraviolet part of the spectrum. Regardless, the eyes of deer are highly adapted to low-light vision, much more so than people. They are also significantly more attuned to motion detection. A deer won't detect a person's presence on the basis of a bright orange shirt, even at close range; but if he or she so much as wiggles a finger, it will be seen immediately.

The extent to which whitetail deer rely upon the nose to detect predators and locate food sources is difficult to exaggerate. The nose of a wolf contains an estimated three hundred million olfactory receptors compared to six million in the snoot of the average human. Its brain dedicates forty times as much area to processing scent stimuli as a person's. Ungulate species, including whitetail deer and elk, are equally impressive in their olfactory abilities. It is estimated that the twitching black nose of a whitetail connects to a scent-sifting apparatus that is one thousand times more sensitive than a human's. What's more, a deer can detect and analyze multiple smells simultaneously.

Vocal and Visual Communication

Whitetail deer communicate with a variety of noises, sounds discerned by their fuzzy ears. Research performed on the auditory capabilities of deer has shown they hear best at the same tonal range as humans. However, they are capable of hearing high-pitched sounds undetectable to a person.

Whether listening for the grunt of a rival buck or the crunch of a hiker's foot on gravel, the ears of a whitetail are significantly more sophisticated than a human's. They are proportionally much larger. Their elongated dish shape makes them very effective in capturing sound waves. Whitetails can swivel their ears independently to maximize their hearing in a particular direction.

Alert to a noise behind her, this doe in Great Smoky Mountains National Park has swiveled her ears, an ability that helps whitetails pinpoint the source of sound. LISA BALLARD

A deer's ears are important to detecting danger but also are used to receive communication from their own kind. Whitetails make a variety of sounds at various stages of life and at different times of the year. Does grunt softly to their newborn fawns. Fawns emit what is sometimes described as a murmuring sound when nursing. A fawn separated from its mother may signal its apprehension with a very loud bleating noise.

Bucks communicate vocally during the mating season, which occurs in the fall. Their calls are mostly grunt-like, with variations communicating certain activities or emotions. Bucks may grunt when following the scent of a doe. They also grunt to warn other bucks away when tending a doe.

Deer of both sexes may emit a loud snort when alarmed. A loud, lower-pitched snort alerts other deer to danger, but isn't an immediate signal to flee. If the snorting deer resorts to an even more intense, higher-pitched snort, other deer will instantly take flight, knowing a real threat is at hand.

The physical postures of whitetails communicate to other deer, similar to one person reading the body language of another. If a deer becomes alert, raising its head and staring intently in a particular direction, other deer in the area will also become alert. Deer may also stomp their feet when aroused by potential danger, a behavior that sends both an audible and visual signal to other whitetails. On one fall outing, I sat near a trail high in the mountains of Montana eating a sandwich. Between bites I heard the stomp of a hoof behind me. Although it was much higher in the mountains than I expected to encounter whitetails, I knew the sound. I turned my head very slowly to see a young whitetail buck staring at me from just a few paces away. My direct eye contact prompted a high-pitched snort and the buck bounded away.

Herd Behavior

Whitetail deer are not herd animals in the same sense as bison, which often form large, fairly intact groups. In the winter, many whitetails may be found together in a confined wintering area, but their proximity to one another is a function of habitat, not a

Except during the mating season, whitetail bucks often live together in small herds.

herding instinct. However, whitetails usually spend much of the year together in one of two kinds of small groups.

The first is a maternal group. Does commonly stay in a small band with their mother and her other offspring until they are around three years of age. The does in this family group become solitary when birthing their fawns, but they rejoin the band once the fawns have reached a few weeks of age. When a person observes several doe deer together with their fawns, the odds are quite high that they are all related through the dominant doe or "grandmother" of the group.

The second type of whitetail "herd" is the male group or bachelor band. Except during the mating season, whitetail bucks normally live together in groups of a few animals up to a

Whitetails often raise their tail when alarmed and hold it erect when fleeing danger. Biologists believe this alerts other deer to danger and discourages predators from pursuit.

WHAT TO MAKE OF A WAVING WHITE TAIL?

The most dramatic form of body language initiated by the whitetail is the raising of its white tail when it is alert or fleeing danger. When startled, deer often raise their tail above their rump. As they flee, it waves like a white flag.

Biologists believe the waving tail serves two purposes. First, it alerts other deer in the vicinity of danger. Secondly, it sends a clear message to a predator that says, "I've seen you, so it's now a waste of your time to chase me."

Not all deer raise their tails when alarmed or on the run. Bucks tend to flash their tail less than does. Individual deer seem to vary in their willingness to elevate their tail. But the message is the same. A deer with its tail raised has already sensed danger and won't be an easy target for any predator, be it a wolf or human hunter.

dozen or more, depending on the density of deer in a particular area. Bucks typically join these bands as yearlings and may associate with the same core group for several years. Biologists theorize that living together in small groups gives both males and females extra eyes and ears when it comes to predator detection. It's not terribly unusual to encounter single whitetails, but small-herd life is the norm.

CHAPTER 5 Reproduction and Young

The Mating Season

For people intrigued with whitetail deer, whether photographers, hunters, or wildlife watchers, the mating season is one of the highlights of the year. Also known as the rut, the mating season creates a spike in deer activity. Bucks invisible at other times may show themselves during the rut. The whitetail world is alive with magnificent animals in prime physical condition, engaging in rituals of reproduction as ancient as the species itself.

The timing of the whitetail rut varies with location. In southern climates the start, length, and predictability of the mating season are less certain than in the north. The primary trigger for the rut is the photoperiod, or the length of daylight. As daylight diminishes during the fall in the northern United States and Canada, it stimulates hormonal shifts in whitetails that prompt reproductive behaviors. Seasonal changes in the photoperiod aren't as significant as one moves south, leading to a less-defined mating season. Near the equator, whitetail deer may mate and birth young at any time of the year.

For northern whitetails, the breeding season typically lasts around a month, with most of the mating occurring in a twenty-day period. Breeding may occur for several weeks on either side of the peak period, which commonly occurs in November. In my home state of Montana, mating behaviors tend to be most intense during the last two weeks of November.

In the southern United States, the mating season is longer and lacks the intense period associated with northern whitetails. Researchers have identified September as the month of peak breeding activity in portions of South Carolina. In Alabama and Mississippi, December is typically the peak month. Whitetails in northern Florida often mate most frequently in March, while deer in the southern portion of the state commonly breed in July.

In northern climates, the whitetail deer mating season commonly occurs in November.

Whitetails engage in a mating pattern known in biological circles as a tending-bond system. This simply refers to the habitat of a single buck courting a single doe until she is ready for mating. The buck will repel other bucks from her presence and will also attempt to keep the doe from fleeing his advances. Once the doe has been bred, the buck moves on, seeking another female with which to mate.

This buck is preparing to rub his antlers in Shenandoah National Park. Rubs serve as territorial markers for bucks during the rut.

The actual mating season includes a prelude in which bucks advertise their status both to does and rival males. Increased testosterone levels cause the necks of mature bucks to swell to the point where they may look more like a thick-necked bull than a sleek deer. For several weeks before the rut and during the mating period, bucks rub their antlers vigorously on small trees and brush, creating what is often called a rub. As the buck thrashes his antlers on a tree trunk or willow brush, scent from a system of glands on his head and face are left on the bark. Other deer obtain information on this vigor based on the odor. The rub also serves as a visual signal to other animals. Bucks often create rubs that follow something of a trail or line, indicating their claim on the area as their home territory.

A similar form of communication is found in places where bucks paw the ground before or during the rut. These are known as scrapes and usually appear as a patch of bare earth amid a ground cover of fallen leaves, grass, or other vegetation. Scrapes are often located beneath an overhanging tree branch. In addition to pawing the ground, the buck rubs his head on the overhanging limb and may also nibble on its twigs. Scrapes are another way bucks advertise their territory during the rut. Other bucks, both subordinates and rivals, may visit the scrape of another. The scent and signals left after a visit serve as "business cards" identifying a buck's relative age and status. It is quite likely that deer can identify one another purely on the basis of scent. Confronted with the scent markings of the dominant buck in a territory at a scrape, a subordinate is probably quite aware of his superior.

Most often, bucks do not need to fight to establish which one is dominant and thus will have the mating rights to a doe. However, bucks evenly matched in size and perceived status will battle. The confrontation commences with the bucks staring directly at each other and circling, with each displaying his body and antler size to his opponent. Other signs of aggression include raised hair on the back and neck and ears laid back flat. If neither backs down during this mutual intimidation session, the fight begins when they clash their antlers together at close range.

A scrape in Custer State Park, South Dakota, where whitetails are abundant, shows evidence of a rutting buck. Lisa Ballard

If one buck substantially outmatches the other, the fight will last for just a few seconds before one male breaks away. Closely matched bucks may battle until they are nearly exhausted. Fighting strategies attempt to throw a rival from his feet or twist him sideways. Both tactics are designed to give a buck the opportunity to gore his opponent with his antlers. Intense battles may leave both victor and vanquished with lacerated ears, puncture wounds, joint injuries, and blinded eyes. Fights between bucks are spectator events in the whitetail world. Other bucks, and sometimes does, are attracted to the sound of crashing antlers during a fight and may travel considerable distances to witness the battle.

Pregnancy and Gestation

The gestation period, or time between breeding and birthing, for whitetail deer is around 200 days. Gestations between 187 and 213 days have been observed in whitetails. At a six-and-a-half month average, this means a doe that mated in Montana's Glacier National Park in late November will birth her fawn in mid-June. The relatively brief mating season of northern deer means most fawns will be born within a short period of time that spans just a few weeks. This phenomenon, known as synchronous breeding, has certain survival advantages. Numerous predators are capable of killing a whitetail fawn. When most of the year's young are born in a short period of time, it contracts the period in which they can be successfully hunted, allowing more to survive.

The age and nutritional status of a doe are highly instrumental in her pregnancy. Whitetail fawns may breed before they reach one year of age, but they normally do so later in the mating season than adult does. Both female fawns and yearlings usually birth a single fawn. Adult does with good nutrition typically have twins, sometimes triplets. Does birthing up to five offspring have been recorded, though the birth of more than three fawns is very rare.

Caused by long, severe winters, summer drought, or marginal habitat, malnourishment is an important factor in pregnancy

Twins are commonly born to whitetail does. These healthy twins are prepared to face their first winter.

rates. Under normal habitat conditions, whitetail does in the northeastern United States have conception rates of 85 to 95 percent. Pregnancy rates are similar elsewhere in the country where deer have access to good forage. Does entering the breeding season in poor physical condition with low fat reserves are far less likely to become pregnant.

Birth

About a week before giving birth, whitetail does retreat to a birthing area. Does attempt to repel other deer from this territory, even their young from the previous year. Her most recent fawns, now yearlings, are forcibly removed from the area with kicks and other aggressive behaviors.

Does hide their newborn fawns in a secure area. For several days they will only tend the fawn for brief times to nurse.

The birth of the fawn is preceded by her udder swelling with milk, around two days before the birth takes place. Birth usually begins with the doe lying on her side but is often completed in a standing position. Healthy fawns succeed in standing within thirty minutes of birth and nurse shortly thereafter. Fawns from undernourished does may lack the energy to stand and then starve. Does vigorously lick their newborn fawns, cleaning them of birthing fluids and tissues, and stimulating them to move and stand. Twin fawns born to healthy does are delivered within thirty minutes of each other. Whitetail fawns have white spots on their coats that disappear when their baby coat is shed in early autumn.

Some hours after birth, the doe will lead her fawns (or fawn) away from the birthing area. She then oversees them while they

This doe and her young fawn have been joined by her previous year's offspring, which was briefly allowed to nurse, a rather unusual behavior.

lie down in separate locations. Once the fawns are settled, the doe retreats to her own spot, some distance from the fawns. Biologists theorize this practice reduces the odds of a predator scenting the birthing area and finding the fawns. For the next few weeks, the doe will attend to her fawns for only a few times per day when they nurse. At a bit less than a month of age, the doe and her fawns will again mingle with her previous year's offspring and other members of the maternal group.

Nurturing Fawns to Adulthood

One of the most critical periods in a fawn's survival is the first week of life. Very young fawns are easy targets for predators. However, due to their inactivity and the fact that they are nearly scentless,

This two-month-old fawn is fast enough to foil most predators. It has survived some of the most precarious days of its life. Lisa Ballard

predators have a difficult time discovering them. A month-old fawn is fleet of foot. It can outrun many potential predators and may be defended by its mother if attacked. Its mobility is also a liability. Numerous research projects indicate fawns are most susceptible to predators between two and nine weeks of age. Young whitetails that reach three months of age are less likely to be preyed upon.

How important is it for a fawn to evade predators? In populations where natural predators are present in average or above-average numbers, predation is the leading cause of mortality in whitetail fawns. It is not unusual for predators to consume over 50 percent of the local fawn crop in a given year. Vehicle collisions, malnourishment, accidents, and diseases may also cut into the year's class of fawns. However, whitetails have a notably high reproductive rate. Whitetail populations that have declined due to disease or winter mortality can recover in a matter of a few years.

Once a fawn has reached the age where it is able to elude most predators, it still faces several challenges before reaching adulthood. A whitetail's first winter can be a major survival hurdle. If cold temperatures and deep snow persist, the youngest deer are among the first to succumb to starvation. Their smaller body size makes them less able to fight the cold. Where browse is scarce, young deer cannot reach as high onto shrubs and trees to nibble twigs. Fawns also find it more difficult to navigate deep snow. Once weakened, they are also easier targets for large predators such as wolves and mountain lions.

Yearling deer, especially bucks, often disperse from the home range of their mother to live in new territory. These movements can create hazards, including highway crossings, unknown predators, and hostile members of their own kind. However, once a deer has survived its first birthday, it is well on the road to adulthood.

ISSUES AND WHITETAILS

LET THEM LIE

Each year, wildlife officials are confronted with people who have "rescued" a fawn they found abandoned in a field or forest. In the vast majority of cases, the fawn wasn't an orphan. Its mother was in the vicinity, but like other does, she returned to her offspring only a few times a day to nurse it.

If you find a young fawn by itself, leave it alone. Its mother is probably caring for it. If you handle it, the doe may actually abandon it due to the human scent you leave behind. For the sake of the fawn, let it lie.

CHAPTER 6 Whitetail Deer and Other Animals

Whitetails and Other Ungulates

In many parts of the country, whitetail deer are found on the same ranges as other North American members of the deer family: elk, moose, and mule deer. They may also inhabit prairie habitats shared with pronghorn, although whitetails normally select niche areas on the plains (creek bottoms, wooded draws) that are used less frequently by pronghorn. In a handful of locations, whitetail deer may come into contact with bighorn sheep on winter range and, to a lesser extent, mountain goats. However, their most regular interactions with other ungulates are shared with other members of the deer species.

Whitetails are incapable of directly challenging a larger moose or elk for forage or space. The interactions between these species are generally peaceful, with the smaller giving way to the larger. However, under some circumstances each may consume the same food sources, creating direct or indirect competition for forage. This most likely occurs in the northern portion of whitetail range in locations such as Idaho, Wyoming, Montana, and southern Canada.

In one study, researchers analyzed the winter diets of whitetail deer, elk, and moose in northwestern Montana. Dietary overlap was minimal during mild or normal winters, but one severe winter saw all three species consuming high percentages of the same forage. Under such circumstances whitetails are at a disadvantage compared to their larger relatives and may experience nutritional stress locally due to such competition. However, in general the long-term health of a whitetail deer population is not thought to be diminished by the presence of elk or moose.

Whitetails, though, may impact moose populations. Whitetail deer are often hosts to meningeal worms (brainworms). These

In severe winters whitetails may compete with elk for forage in some locations.

parasites normally don't cause problems for deer but are deadly to moose. Moose are often absent in areas of high whitetail deer densities, even in good habitat. Many biologists theorize the presence of so many deer increases the odds of meningeal worm infection in moose to the point they are unable to survive.

Whitetails and their closest North American relative, the mule deer, share habitat in numerous regions throughout the United States and Canada. While mule deer are generally a creature of more open spaces and roam at higher elevations in the Rocky Mountains, there is considerable overlap in the range of the two species in both mountain, prairie, and river-bottom habitats.

Over the past few decades, mule deer numbers have declined in most places in the West. The reasons aren't fully known, but in some areas biologists speculate whitetail deer, whose numbers are generally increasing, may be instrumental in the decline. White-tails are thought to be a more aggressive species and may displace mule deer in direct competition for food or other resources. It is important to remember, however, that correlation (observing two things are related) does not necessarily imply causation (one thing caused the other). While many people have pointed to increasing whitetail deer numbers as a cause for diminishing mule deer numbers, this hypothesis has not been confirmed or denied by scientific research.

An interesting twist in the relationship between whitetail and mule deer is their ability to interbreed. Crossbred animals of the two species are exceedingly rare in the wild, but in areas where they share the same range, some interspecies mating may occur. It is believed by many commentators that hybrids are usually the offspring of a whitetail buck and a mule deer doe, although that theory has not been verified by research on wild deer. What is known is that the survival of hybrid fawns is very low, even in captivity. Several captive breeding programs of these hybrid deer have a survival rate in fawns of around 50 percent.

Hybrids of the species inherit characteristics of both species and are extremely hard to identify in the wild. They generally have ears that are shorter than a mule deer's but longer than a whitetail's. Their tails are typically long, with dark fur on the outside and white hair on the underside in the pattern of a whitetail, but they often display much darker outer fur than is normally seen with whitetails. Survival of hybrids is possibly confounded by a mixing of the two gaits characteristic of each species. Mule deer run in a so-called stotting fashion, which means they bound with all four hooves hitting the ground at the same time in what appears as a pogo-stick or bouncing movement. Whitetails gallops similar to a running horse. Some evidence exists that hybrids inherit an awkward gait that may make them much less efficient in fleeing predators than either of their parents.

The only positive way to identify a crossbred deer is by examining the metatarsal gland on the outer portion of its lower leg. Mule deer have a metatarsal gland that sits high on the lower portion of

Where their ranges overlap, the relationship between mule deer and whitetails can be complex, including interbreeding of the species.

the leg, measures from about 4 to 6 inches long, and is surrounded by brownish fur. The metatarsal gland of a whitetail is usually less than 1 inch in length, sits just below the midpoint of the lower leg, and is adorned with white fur. The metatarsal gland of a hybrid combines features of both parents. It is noticeably larger than a whitetail's, smaller than a mule deer's, and surrounded by white fur. To a skilled observer, this is the only way to differentiate hybrids, and it applies only to first-generation crossbreeds. First-generation male hybrids are usually sterile, but females are not. Genetic testing shows evidence of a small commingling of whitetail and mule deer genes in some places where their ranges overlap. A study in the early 1980s in western Texas found some evidence of hybridization in about 5 percent of deer from the two species. Results from similar testing in Montana revealed that somewhat less than 2 percent of the deer displayed evidence of hybridization.

Whitetails and Predators

Whitetail deer are important prey for various predators. Predation is a leading cause of mortality in many areas, but the rapid reproduction of the species allows for high levels of predation without causing significant populations declines.

To understand the influence of predators on whitetail deer populations, it is helpful to distinguish between compensatory and additive predation. Compensatory predation occurs when animals of a species killed by predators would have died to other causes. Deer cannot be stockpiled like canned food. A particular area can only support a finite number of whitetails. As their population increases, malnutrition, winter starvation, vehicle collisions, parasites, and diseases all claim varying numbers of deer each year. Compensatory predation occurs when predators such as wolves simply consume deer that would have been lost to some other factor. In good habitat conditions with normal numbers of deer and predators, biologists believe that predation is primarily compensatory.

Additive predation takes place when predators kill enough animals within a species that their influence adds to, instead of replaces, other types of mortality. Current research suggests this type of predation occurs with whitetails in areas with low populations, either as a function of habitat or after some dramatic event such as an exceptionally hard winter has severely reduced deer numbers. It appears predation can be a limiting factor in herd growth among whitetail deer in such instances.

The two species of predators that routinely prey on whitetails throughout the year in North America are mountain lions and wolves. Studies in both the northern and southern Rocky Mountains have shown deer (both whitetails and mule deer) compose the bulk of the typical mountain lion's diet. Some research indicates that where both species of deer exist, mountain lion predation on mule deer is disproportionately higher than on whitetails.

The predator-prey relationship between mountain lions and whitetails is complex. Female mountain lions consume more whitetails than males where other larger prey, such as elk and moose, are present. Biologists theorize that, because of the smaller size of the female cats, deer are a more manageable prey than bigger animals. Mountain lions prey heavily on whitetail fawns in the first few months of life, but other age classes of deer are vulnerable at certain times of the year. Research has shown that predation on does increases just prior to and after the birthing period. Older bucks are killed at higher rates after the mating season due to their physically stressed condition.

Wolves are another year-round and important predator of whitetail deer. Wolf predation on whitetails occurs primarily in the Great Lakes region, southern Canada, and the northern Rocky Mountains. Like other predators, wolves avidly consume whitetail fawns in the first few months of life. Their predation on whitetails may also increase during the winter. In open territory where deer can see for long distances, wolves have low odds of catching a whitetail. One study in Montana discovered wolves killed more deer in heavy cover and where deer densities were low. This possibly indicates that multiple deer are better at detecting wolves and more capable of escape in sparse cover.

Wolves are among the predators that routinely prey upon whitetails year-round. Lisa Ballard

Wolves prey heavily on adult deer as well as fawns in some places. A long-term study in Minnesota revealed that wolves killed between 4 and 22 percent of the doe deer in four study areas per year. The highest percentage occurred during a very severe winter when deep snows and weakened deer made them easy targets for wolves.

Coyotes may prey on whitetails (especially fawns) and are a significant source of deer mortality in many regions in the eastern United States. Coyotes were historically an animal primarily of the western plains but have colonized much of the East in the past five decades. Compared to their western counterparts, eastern coyotes are typically larger because of the genetic influence of coyote-wolf hybrids from eastern Canada and the north-central United States. Research in Pennsylvania concluded that

Coyotes can capably prey upon whitetails, especially fawns, and are their number-one predator in many parts of the eastern United States.

the recently arrived coyotes had an additive predatory effect on whitetail populations, primarily in relation to fawn production. Human hunting is the primary means by which whitetail deer populations are kept from increasing to habitat-destructive levels in most parts of the country. Coyote predation in parts of the East has pressured populations to the extent that the number of doe deer harvested by hunters will apparently need to be reduced to accommodate the additional predation of coyotes.

A number of other predators have the ability to prey upon whitetails and may have a regional or local impact on mortality. These include bobcats and grizzly and black bears. In some places, bobcats are a significant predator of whitetail fawns. Studies in the southeastern United States have shown regional predation rates of bobcats at 7 percent (South Carolina), 8 percent (Alabama), and

9 percent (Georgia) of the total yearly fawn crop. Grizzly bears and black bears also opportunistically prey upon fawns and may be a substantial source of mortality in some places.

Other creatures such as red foxes, gray foxes, wolverines, Canada lynx, bald eagles, and golden eagles infrequently prey upon whitetails. Although predation of whitetails (mostly fawns) has been documented among these creatures, it is considered very rare.

Parasites and Diseases

Over one hundred different internal parasites have been recorded in whitetail deer in the United States. These run the gamut from tapeworms to lungworms to liver flukes. In most cases these parasites do not noticeably affect a deer's health. Heavy infestations of such parasites can lead to malnutrition or death, and they often occur when deer overpopulate their range. Heavy concentrations of lungworms, for example, are most common in young deer in stressed or poor habitat and can lead to weight loss or, in severe cases, death.

External parasites can be bothersome to whitetails and in rare cases can be fatal. Heavy tick infestations cause fawn mortality in some places. Along with ticks, deer are susceptible to biting flies, midges, and mosquitoes. They also serve as host to nasal bots, larvae of the *Cephenemyia* fly. The larvae invade a deer's nasal cavity and may be found at the back of the mouth. They are extremely bothersome and may stimulate aggressive sneezing or blowing when a deer tries to expel the pests.

Deer ticks, very small ticks common to whitetails, do not normally create problems for the deer. However, these are the carriers of Lyme disease, a malady that, if left untreated, is often fatal to humans. High numbers of whitetails in urban areas are thus a health concern in some places given their potential to host Lyme-spreading ticks. Other creatures such as rodents and birds can also carry the tick, so eliminating deer from an area may lower human exposure to Lyme disease but will not eliminate it.

External parasites on this doe's head at Great Smoky Mountains National Park may be what prompts her scratching. Deer are bothered by many external parasites, but only in rare cases are they harmful to an animal's health.

Whitetails suffer from a host of diseases, most of which cause only temporary discomfort to the animal. However, some diseases are much more serious. In the United States, the most important of these are hemorrhagic diseases, chronic wasting disease, and bovine tuberculosis.

Hemorrhagic diseases include epizootic hemorrhagic disease (EHD) and blue tongue, which includes several strains. These viral infections are spread among deer by biting midges. They cause internal bleeding and are often fatal. Hemorrhagic disease occurs regularly in the southern United States and is becoming increasingly common in the north. Southern deer appear less susceptible to the disease. Farther north, outbreaks can cause severe losses of whitetail deer in some locations. These diseases are often associated with water and usually peak in late summer, when biting midges are most prevalent. The presence of deer carcasses near streams or standing water in late summer is a strong indication of a hemorrhagic disease outbreak.

Chronic wasting disease (CWD) is a variant of mad cow disease. It affects the brain and nervous system when proteins called prions alter the composition of a deer's brain. CWD is fatal to deer. Infected deer become malnourished, lose their ability to walk normally, and die. The disease is spread most readily by animal-to-animal contact, particularly in the saliva. Other means of transmission may also be possible.

Bovine tuberculosis (TB) is not present in deer in high numbers, but it is a concern in relation to its potential transmission to livestock. TB is a slowly progressing respiratory disease that deer or other animals may carry for years. It is not always fatal. TB may cause great economic loss among cattle operations, thus the intense concern regarding TB in deer. Whitetails in Michigan are known to host the disease, which may occur elsewhere in the country.

CHAPTER 7 Whitetails and Humans

Whitetails and American Indians

Whitetail deer were an important source of food, clothing, and tools for native peoples of North America for thousands of years before the arrival of European settlers. Archaeological evidence from Texas indicates native hunters pursued whitetails at least ten thousand years prior to the present era. Whitetail bones have been found in numerous archaeological sites. Near San Antonio, excavation for dam construction in the late 1970s uncovered a burial site. Whitetail deer antlers were carefully arranged over the graves, indicating some association with deer and the afterlife. Analysis of whitetail bones from archaeological excavations also suggests that the Texas whitetails of prehistoric times were significantly larger than they are today.

Before they acquired firearms from Europeans, American Indians used numerous ingenious methods to hunt whitetails. Perhaps the most basic technique was the still hunt, in which hunters moved carefully through deer habitat in an attempt to spot and stalk within archery range of deer. The bows and arrows used to hunt deer and other large animals were strong and deadly. One European hunter observed the bow of an Indian hunter propelling an arrow halfway through the body cavity of a deer at a range of 40 yards.

It is extremely difficult to approach a wary whitetail within archery range. To counteract their quarry's acute senses, native hunters often hid near established deer trails to ambush them. Stacked stones used to hide waiting hunters were placed within bow range of deer trails by Midwestern tribes. They also lured deer into archery range with various vocal calls and by clashing antlers together to simulate a buck fight. Native hunters sometimes wore stalks of grass on their heads to disguise their approach in grassy cover.

Native hunters hid along established deer trails, like this one in Montana, to ambush traveling whitetails.

The Powhatan tribe that occupied territory in Virginia was among the first group of natives encountered by early settlers. Historical accounts of their hunting methods indicate deer were encircled by a band of torch-wielding hunters who drove the animals to the center. As the circle tightened, hunters were able to get close enough to kill them. Whitetails were also driven into water and then dispatched from canoes. Another method involved hunters draping themselves in a single deer hide with a stuffed head and stalking the quarry within bow range.

Whitetails and European Settlers

Colonists arriving in the New World found two ready uses for whitetail deer: Their meat and fat became an important source of food and their hides a valued item of trade. Some historians speculate that trade with the colonists in the seventeenth and eighteenth centuries prompted native peoples to kill more deer strictly for their hides than they had in previous times. Increasing numbers of European hunters and the acquisition of firearms by Indians eventually led to conditions in which whitetail reproduction could not keep pace with the harvest.

A plague among European cattle in the early eighteenth century prompted England to ban the import of cattle or their hides from Europe. To meet the demand for leather, deer hides from the American colonies became an extremely valuable commodity. Deer hides flowed to England primarily through the ports at Charleston, South Carolina, and Savannah, Georgia. Historical records indicate that from 1699 to 1715 the port of Charleston shipped around 54,000 deerskins to England per year. As demand increased, hunting of whitetails intensified. Shipping records from Charleston verify well over 5 million pounds of deer hides were exported from 1739 to 1761. From 1755 to 1772, around 2.5 million pounds of deerskins passed through the port at Savannah. In 1748 an estimated 160,000 deerskins were exported from the colonies. John Stuart, southern superintendent for Indian affairs, stated in 1764 that the number had grown to approximately 400,000 hides per year.

Deer hides were an important commodity in colonial trade with England. Hides from large bucks like this beauty in Shenandoah National Park commanded the highest value.

Before hunting pressure reduced whitetail numbers, trade in deerskins gave the members of various American Indian tribes access to a host of desirable goods. A 1717 agreement between the colonists and the Cherokee tribe specified the price of a musket (a primitive firearm) would be thirty-five deer hides. Bullets for the musket could be had at the rate of thirty per hide. A single deerskin could buy a knife, and three skins fetched a hatchet. A similar contract from 1751 underscores the increasing scarcity of deer hides. It specifies different terms for buck hides (larger) versus those of does (smaller). At that time, a gun could be acquired with seven buck hides or fourteen doe skins. A single doe hide could be exchanged for thirty bullets.

Market hunting for whitetails occurred at various levels of intensity and across numerous regions of the country until the close of the nineteenth century. By this time whitetails were very scarce or extinct over much of their historic range. But in 1900 the Lacey Act, a federal law prohibiting the interstate shipment of wildlife, including deer meat and hides, became law. Shortly thereafter many state legislatures created wildlife agencies and adopted hunting seasons or increased restrictions on deer harvests via existing seasons.

Whitetails and Us

Strict regulation of deer hunting, habitat changes involving timber harvest and clearing of forest for agriculture, and the reintroduction of deer to establish or bolster existing populations saw whitetail numbers increase throughout most of the United States during the early and mid-1900s. For example, by the 1930s deer numbers in northern Pennsylvania had increased to the point of intense habitat destruction in many locations. Unchecked whitetail populations can reduce or eliminate many plant species and desirable trees and shrubs. The middle decades of the 1900s saw overprotection of deer in numerous regions have substantially negative impacts on the ecosystem.

Throughout the early decades of the twentieth century, hunting seasons in most states generally protected does and allowed only the harvest of bucks. By the end of the 1970s, wildlife managers increasingly acknowledged the need for human hunters to kill does to keep deer numbers in check in the absence of major natural predators in most places.

Although no one knows for sure, many whitetail experts believe there are at least as many whitetail deer currently in the United States as there were in precolonial times. Estimates vary, but it is commonly believed around thirty million whitetails track the forests, fields, and even cities of the United States and Canada.

Human hunting is critical to keeping whitetail deer numbers in balance with their habitat capacity in most parts of the country. The return of wolves to the northern Rocky Mountains, the expansion of mountain lion populations in the West, and growing numbers of coyotes in the East have added a natural balancing component to whitetail herds in some places. However, without the harvest of whitetails by hunters, the deer would soon

Human hunting is essential to maintain healthy whitetail populations in most parts of the country.

proverbially "eat themselves out of house and home" in most parts of the country.

Human hunters harvest around six million deer annually in the United States. In Texas, well over one million deer-hunting licenses are sold each year. Whitetail deer are the most popular big game animal in the United States, with over eleven million hunters pursuing the species each year. The sale of deer-hunting licenses is an integral component of most state wildlife agency

ISSUES AND WHITETAILS

DEER DAMAGE

Whitetails are a driving force in the economies of state wildlife agencies and outdoor recreation. However, they also cause significant economic loss. A survey of thirteen northeastern states concluded whitetails caused $248 million annually in damages to landscaping, nurseries, and crops. Degradation of habitat through overbrowsing by whitetails negatively affects plant communities and can suppress the presence of other wildlife species.

Although exact numbers are not available (as not all vehicle collisions with deer are reported), in 2008 the Insurance Institute for Highway Safety pegged whitetail collisions with motorized vehicles at around one million nationwide. It is generally accepted that deer-vehicle accidents cause around $1 billion in damages per year. Wildlife advocates have promoted deer-proof fencing with above or below highway crossings for deer and other species where highway collisions are numerous, but such solutions are expensive. However, weighed simply against the cost of collisions to both property and human life (150 people died in collisions with deer in 2008, some 29,000 were injured), projects to reduce vehicle accidents with deer and other wildlife may prove a worthwhile long-term investment.

Whitetails have economic value in many ways. This curious doe is part of what attracts tourists to places like her home in Glacier National Park. LISA BALLARD

Whitetails are remarkable in their ability to adapt to changing environments. The future outlook for the species, like this buck in Custer State Park, South Dakota, is excellent.
LISA BALLARD

budgets. It is estimated that whitetail hunting contributes $6 billion to the United States economy each year. Estimates indicate that nearly 300 million pounds of venison (deer meat) are consumed as a result of whitetail hunting each year.

However, the value of our most widespread large mammal isn't restricted to hunting. Whitetails are a popular part of the wildlife-viewing experience in many national parks such as Great Smoky Mountains and Shenandoah. They're a popular attraction at hundreds of state parks, national monuments, and other preserves across the country.

Whitetails have been introduced in parts of Europe and are considered to be perhaps the most widely distributed ungulate in the world. They have shown a remarkable ability to adapt to human civilization and are considered to be one of the large mammals most capable of thriving in the future age of climate change and increasing pressure on natural resources.

Index

About the Author

A writer, photographer, and naturalist, Jack Ballard is a frequent contributor to numerous regional and national publications. He has written hundreds of articles on wildlife and wildlife-related topics.

His photos have been published in numerous books (Smithsonian Press, Heinemann Library, etc.), calendars, and magazines. Jack has received multiple awards for his writing and photography from the Outdoor Writers Association of America and other professional organizations. He holds two master's degrees and is an accomplished public speaker, entertaining students, conference attendees, and recreation/conservation groups with his compelling narratives. When not wandering the backcountry, he hangs his hat in Red Lodge, Montana. See more of his work at jackballard.com.